STATES

ARKANSAS

A MyReportLinks.com Book

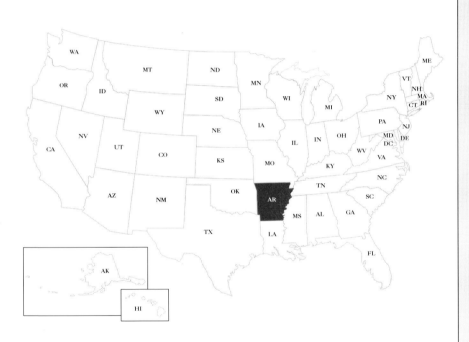

Marylou Morano Kjelle

MyReportLinks.com Books

an imprint of

 Enslow Publishers, Inc.

Box 398, 40 Industrial Road
Berkeley Heights, NJ 07922
USA

MyReportLinks.com Books, an imprint of Enslow Publishers, Inc. MyReportLinks is a trademark of Enslow Publishers, Inc.

Library of Congress Cataloging-in-Publication Data

Kjelle, Marylou Morano.
 Arkansas / Marylou Morano Kjelle.
 p. cm. — (States)
 Summary: Discusses the land and climate, economy, government, and history of the state of Arkansas. Includes Internet links to Web sites.
 Includes bibliographical references (p.) and index.
 ISBN 0-7660-5152-8
 1. Arkansas—Juvenile literature. [1. Arkansas.] I. Title. II. States
(Series : Berkeley Heights, N.J.)
 F411.3 .K58 2003
 976.7—dc21

                              2002153561

Printed in the United States of America

10 9 8 7 6 5 4 3 2 1

To Our Readers:
Through the purchase of this book, you and your library gain access to the Report Links that specifically back up this book.
The Publisher will provide access to the Report Links that back up this book and will keep these Report Links up to date on **www.myreportlinks.com** for three years from the book's first publication date.
We have done our best to make sure all Internet addresses in this book were active and appropriate when we went to press. However, the author and the Publisher have no control over, and assume no liability for, the material available on those Internet sites or on other Web sites they may link to.
The usage of the MyReportLinks.com Books Web site is subject to the terms and conditions stated on the Usage Policy Statement on **www.myreportlinks.com**.
A password may be required to access the Report Links that back up this book. The password is found on the bottom of page 4 of this book.
Any comments or suggestions can be sent by e-mail to comments@myreportlinks.com or to the address on the back cover.

Photo Credits: Arkansas Department of Parks & Tourism, pp. 13, 20, 23 (top); Arkansas Office of Tourism, pp. 23 (bottom), 26, 30; ArtToday.com, pp. 11, 18; © Corel Corporation, pp. 3, 10 (flag), 24, 28; © Canadian Museum of Civilization, p. 39; © 1995 PhotoDisc, pp. 34, 44; © 1998 The Filmmakers Collaborative and The Smithsonian Institution, p. 32; © 1999 PBS/WGBH, p. 15; Enslow Publishers, Inc., pp. 1, 22; Glen Campbell Enterprises © 1996–2002, p. 16; John Oliver Buckley/U.S. Senate, p. 35; Library of Congress, p. 40; MyReportLinks.com Books, p. 4; National Park Service, p. 42; Photograph by Will Counts, p. 43; University of Arkansas, p. 37.

Cover Photo: © 1995 PhotoDisc

Cover Description: Arkansas Capitol Building

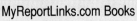
Contents

MyReportLinks.com Books
Great Books, Great Links, Great for Research!

MyReportLinks.com Books present the information you need to learn about your report subject. In addition, they show you where to go on the Internet for more information. The pre-evaluated Report Links that back up this book are kept up to date on **www.myreportlinks.com**. With the purchase of a MyReportLinks.com Books title, you and your library gain access to the Report Links that specifically back up that book. The Report Links save hours of research time and link to dozens—even hundreds—of Web sites, source documents, and photos related to your report topic.

Please see "To Our Readers" on the Copyright page for important information about this book, the MyReportLinks.com Books Web site, and the Report Links that back up this book.

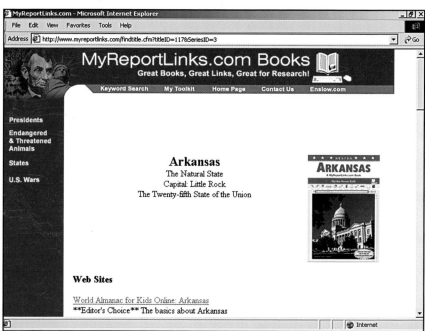

Access:

The Publisher will provide access to the Report Links that back up this book and will try to keep these Report Links up to date on our Web site for three years from the book's first publication date. Please enter **SAR2591** if asked for a password.

*EDITOR'S CHOICE

▶ **World Almanac for Kids Online: Arkansas**
The *World Almanac for Kids Online* Web site contains an overview of
vital Arkansas state facts. Here you will find information about land
and resources, population, education and cultural activity, government
and politics, economy, and history.
Link to this Internet site from http://www.myreportlinks.com

*EDITOR'S CHOICE

▶ **Old Statehouse Museum**
At the Old Statehouse Museum Web site you can explore Arkansas'
people, history, and culture. Click on "Exhibits" to learn about
changing and permanent exhibits. You can also learn the history of
landmarks in Arkansas by clicking on "General Information."
Link to this Internet site from http://www.myreportlinks.com

*EDITOR'S CHOICE

▶ **Explore the States: Arkansas**
America's Story from America's Library, a Library of Congress Web site,
contains a number of short articles about Arkansas. Topics include the
Ozark Mountains, the Arkansas Folk Festival, Louis Jordan, the Little
Rock Air Force Base Air Show, and more.
Link to this Internet site from http://www.myreportlinks.com

*EDITOR'S CHOICE

▶ **The Explorers**
The Civilizations.ca Web site contains a list of explorers, including
Louis Joliet and Jacques Marquette. Both followed the Mississippi
River from the Wisconsin River to the Arkansas River. Here you
will find biographical information and links.
Link to this Internet site from http://www.myreportlinks.com

*EDITOR'S CHOICE

▶ **U.S. Census Bureau: Arkansas**
This site from the United States Census Bureau contains facts and
figures relating to the state of Arkansas. Here you will find population
demographics, housing information, economic statistics, and more.
Link to this Internet site from http://www.myreportlinks.com

*EDITOR'S CHOICE

▶ **Today In History: The Twenty-fifth State**
American Memory, a Library of Congress Web site, tells the story of
the day Arkansas became the twenty-fifth state. Here you will also
find historic pictures of the state.
Link to this Internet site from http://www.myreportlinks.com

Any comments? Contact us:

▶ **About the State of Arkansas**

This site from the Arkansas secretary of state's office contains state symbols, history, facts, information about the state constitution, a diagram of counties, and more.

Link to this Internet site from http://www.myreportlinks.com

▶ **accessArkansas.org**

At the official state of Arkansas Web site you will find information about the state government, local communities, tourism, and more.

Link to this Internet site from http://www.myreportlinks.com

▶ **American Originals: The Louisiana Purchase**

Present-day Arkansas is a portion of the Louisiana Territory, land that the United States purchased from France in 1803. This online exhibit from the National Archives and Records Administration features the original documents of the Louisiana Purchase.

Link to this Internet site from http://www.myreportlinks.com

▶ **Arkansas Arts Center**

The Arkansas Arts Center is the state's largest cultural institution. At their online home you can view the center's vast collection of paintings, drawings, sculptures, and other media. News, events, and visitor information can also be found here.

Link to this Internet site from http://www.myreportlinks.com

▶ **Arkansas History Commission**

At the Arkansas History Commission Web site you can explore the state's archives where you will find photographs and learn historical facts about the state.

Link to this Internet site from http://www.myreportlinks.com

▶ **Arkansas: The Natural State**

Part of the Arkansas Department of Parks & Tourism, this Web site provides an abundance of information about things to do in Arkansas. Here you can explore the state's history, parks, outdoor sports, and much more.

Link to this Internet site from http://www.myreportlinks.com

▶ **Arkansas Post National Memorial**
The Arkansas Post National Memorial sits on the site of the
first semi-permanent French settlement in the lower Mississippi
River valley. This was also a key location in the Revolutionary
and Civil Wars.

Link to this Internet site from http://www.myreportlinks.com

▶ **Bill Clinton: The "New Democratic" President**
The American President series from PBS provides biographies of
all United States presidents, including President Clinton, a native of
Arkansas. Here you will learn about his life before, during, and after
his presidency.

Link to this Internet site from http://www.myreportlinks.com

▶ **A Biography of Scott Joplin**
Ragtime was a popular genre of American music at the start of the
twentieth century. Scott Joplin was the most notorious ragtime
composer. The Scott Joplin International Ragtime Foundation's
Web site contains this biography of the "king of ragtime writers."

Link to this Internet site from http://www.myreportlinks.com

▶ **Fort Smith National Historical Site**
Fort Smith is a key site in American westward expansion. It played a
role in the Civil War, Indian Wars, Trail of Tears, and life in the Old
West. This Web site from the National Park Service includes history,
visitor information, and much more.

Link to this Internet site from http://www.myreportlinks.com

▶ **Glen Campbell**
Glen Campbell went from backing up artists such as the Beach Boys,
Frank Sinatra, and Elvis Presley to becoming a famous singer and
actor himself. Here you will find his biography, discography, photos,
and more.

Link to this Internet site from http://www.myreportlinks.com

▶ **Hot Springs National Park**
This National Park Service Web site contains information about the
oldest park in the United States' national park system, Hot Springs
National Park. Here you will find park history, visitor information,
and other resources.

Link to this Internet site from http://www.myreportlinks.com

Any comments? Contact us: **comments@myreportlinks.com**

▶ **Life & Times of La Salle**
At the Texas Historical Commission Web site you will learn how René-Robert Cavelier, Sieur de La Salle, claimed the entire Mississippi River basin for France. You will also find information about the life and voyages of the famous French explorer.

Link to this Internet site from http://www.myreportlinks.com

▶ **Little Rock Central High 40th Anniversary**
In 1957, the Arkansas National Guard escorted nine African-American students into Little Rock's Central High against the will of Governor Orvil Faubus. This site is dedicated to the story of these nine brave students.

Link to this Internet site from http://www.myreportlinks.com

▶ **MacArthur**
This PBS American Experience site contains a wealth of resources on General Douglas A. MacArthur, who was born in Little Rock, Arkansas. Here you will find a transcript of this PBS documentary, interviews, speeches, letters, newspaper clippings, soldiers' accounts, maps of famous battles, and much more.

Link to this Internet site from http://www.myreportlinks.com

▶ **The Mississippi River of Song**
The Mississippi River of Song, a PBS Web site, tells the stories of musicians along the Mississippi River. At this Web site you will learn about different genres of music and the artists.

Link to this Internet site from http://www.myreportlinks.com

▶ **NBA: Scottie Pippen**
Scottie Pippen is a basketball star, Olympic gold-medal winner, and author. This site from the National Basketball Association contains Pippen's career highlights, personal facts, statistics, and other resources.

Link to this Internet site from http://www.myreportlinks.com

▶ **The Official Johnny Cash.com**
This is the official site of American music icon Johnny Cash. Born in Arkansas, the eclectic performer went on to become a member of both the Rock and Roll and Country Music halls of fame. Photographs, news, discography, audio clips, and other resources can be found here.

Link to this Internet site from http://www.myreportlinks.com

▶**Once Upon a Time in Arkansas**
PBS's *Frontline* takes an in-depth look into the Whitewater scandal, involving President Clinton and First Lady Hillary Rodham Clinton. Here you will learn about the key players, key documents, interviews, and a chronology of events.

Link to this Internet site from http://www.myreportlinks.com

▶**Ouachita National Forest**
This site from the United States Department of Agriculture Park Service is dedicated to the Ozark, St. Francis, and Ouachita national forests. Park facts, maps, and visitor information can be found here.

Link to this Internet site from http://www.myreportlinks.com

▶**The Ozark Folk Center**
The Ozark Folk Center State Park is dedicated to preserving Ozark heritage. In addition to the mountains, the Blanchard Springs caverns, and other natural wonders, the park is host to numerous folk music events. Here you will find history, visitor information, and more.

Link to this Internet site from http://www.myreportlinks.com

▶**Pea Ridge National Military Park**
The 1862 Civil War Battle of Pea Ridge prevented Missouri from falling into Confederate hands. This Web site from the National Park Service contains a brief description of the battle, park information, and more.

Link to this Internet site from http://www.myreportlinks.com

▶**Toltec Mounds**
The Toltec mounds were originally thought to have been built by the Toltec Indians of Mexico. Here you will learn about the mounds, the people who built them, and the Toltec Mounds Archeological State Park.

Link to this Internet site from http://www.myreportlinks.com

▶**U.S. Senate: Hattie Caraway**
Arkansas' Hattie Caraway was the first woman elected to a full term in the United States Senate. The U.S. Senate Web site contains her biography and John Oliver Buckley's portrait of the pioneering senator.

Link to this Internet site from http://www.myreportlinks.com

▶ **Capital**
Little Rock

▶ **Counties**
75

▶ **Gained Statehood**
June 15, 1836,
the twenty-fifth state

▶ **Population**
2,673,400*

▶ **Flower**
Apple blossom

▶ **Bird**
Mockingbird

▶ **Tree**
Pine

▶ **Gem**
Diamond

▶ **Insect**
Honeybee

▶ **Motto**
Regnat Populus (Latin for
"The People Rule")

▶ **Nickname**
Natural State

▶ **Songs**
"The Arkansas Traveler" (words
by the Arkansas State Song

*Population reflects the 2000 census.

Selection committee and music
by Colonel Sanford Faulkner);
"Arkansas (You Run Deep in
Me)" (words and music by
Wayland Holyfield);
"Oh, Arkansas" (words and music
by Terry Rose and Gary Klaff).

▶ **Flag**
In the center of a red field lies a
white diamond outlined in blue.
In the blue part are twenty-five
white stars, because Arkansas was
the twenty-fifth state to enter the
Union. The diamond itself represents the fact that Arkansas is the
only place in North America
where diamonds have been discovered and mined. Inside of the
white portion of the diamond is
"Arkansas." A blue star sitting
above "Arkansas" represents how
the state was one of the Confederate states. The three blue stars
located beneath the state's name
represent Spain, France, and the
United States—the countries that
at one time or another have held
power over the land.

The Natural State

Clear sparkling lakes, deep gorges, and forest-covered mountains cover the land. The beauty of nature is so abundant in Arkansas that it is called the Natural State. This trapezoid-shaped state, located in the south central part of the United States, is completely landlocked. Louisiana lies to its south, Missouri to its north, Oklahoma and Texas to the west, and Mississippi and Tennessee to its east. The winding Mississippi River forms the state's eastern boundary. Arkansas and its neighbor, Texas, share the city of Texarkana, which is located on the state line. Texarkana has two city governments—one for the part of the city that lies in each state. Its post office straddles the state line and uses the address "Texarkana, Arkansas-Texas."

Arkansas ranks thirty-third in the United States in population, with 2,673,400 residents.[1] Caucasians make up over 80 percent of the state's ethnic background, with the next largest representation by African Americans.

The Ozark Mountains stretch 40,000 square miles, covering parts of Arkansas, Illinois, Missouri, and Oklahoma. Spanning 1,500 to 2,300 feet in height, the Ozarks reach their highest point at the Boston Mountains in northwestern Arkansas.

Hispanic Americans, Asian Americans, and American Indians are some of the other groups of people found in Arkansas. More than 50 percent of Arkansans live in urban areas with populations of 2,500 or more people. Little Rock, the centrally located capital that sits on the south bank of the Arkansas River, is the state's largest city. Fort Smith and Fayetteville in the west, and Jonesboro near the Tennessee border in the east, are also heavily populated urban areas.

With an area covering roughly 53,178 square miles, Arkansas is the twenty-ninth largest state. It is the smallest state west of the Mississippi River other than Hawaii. Arkansas is divided into lowlands and highlands in approximately a northeast to southwest division. The Ozark and Ouachita mountains are located in the central and western parts of the state. Rich soil, oil, and natural gas are some of Arkansas' important natural resources. Arkansas has 2.6 million acres of national forestland through which black bear, deer, muskrat, and bobcats roam.

▶ "Downstream People"

When French explorers Jacques Marquette, a Roman Catholic missionary, and Louis Joliet, a fur trader, paddled down the Mississippi River from the Great Lakes in 1673, they encountered the Quapaw Indians. The French called the Quapaws "Arkansas Indians." *Arkansas* is the French version of a Quapaw word meaning "south wind" or "downstream people."

Around 1541, the Spanish explorer de Soto had explored Arkansas but did not settle the land. In the late 1600s, French explorer René-Robert Cavelier, also known as Sieur de La Salle, claimed the entire Mississippi Valley for France. He named it Louisiana, after King Louis XIV.

Present-day Arkansas was included in the Louisiana Purchase from France in 1803. Once the land was owned by the United States, pioneers headed west to the newly acquired "Land of Opportunity," where they purchased and settled their own land. Arkansas became a territory in 1819 and the twenty-fifth state in 1836. By 1840, the young state had a population of over fifty-five thousand, which included people from every state in the Union as well as several foreign countries.[2]

Many settlers owned small farms, but large cotton plantations were built along the fertile land near the Mississippi and Arkansas rivers. The cotton plantations

▲ Since the first diamond was found at Crater of Diamonds in 1906, over seventy-five thousand of these precious stones have been unearthed from the thirty-seven-acre field. Crater of Diamonds became a state park in 1972.

depended upon slavery for their productivity, and Arkansas joined the Confederacy during the Civil War.

Scenic Areas

Arkansas has many natural places to visit. There are six national parks and fifty-one state parks. The Ouachita Mountains are the state's top tourist attraction. Hot mineral springs are found throughout the Ozark and Ouachita mountains. Hot Springs National Park in the Ouachitas is surrounded by Hot Springs, a resort community once called the "Valley of the Vapors" by the area's American Indians. The area contains forty-seven naturally occurring hot mineral springs, the waters of which give off steam as it collects in pools. Many believe the water has healing powers.

Because of their natural beauty, the Ozark and Ouachita mountains and the Arkansas Valley between them are favorite travel destinations for those who enjoy fishing, camping, and cavern exploration. Ozark National Forest contains more than one million acres of lakes, rivers, and scenic mountains. Blanchard Springs Caverns located in the Ozark Mountains is one of the United States' largest cavern systems. Visitors can walk a "Discovery Trail," tour cave rooms, or see a cave stream. Petit Jean State Park, located on the eastern end of the Arkansas Valley, was Arkansas' first state park. It boasts canyons, waterfalls, caves, and springs.

Perhaps the most unusual place in all of Arkansas is Crater of Diamonds State Park. Here visitors can mine for diamonds and other precious gems, such as amethyst, garnet, and quartz. Miners may keep what they find. Since the land was first mined in 1906, more than seventy-five thousand diamonds have been dug up.[3]

Arkansan Contributions

Arkansans have made many contributions to the American way of life. Two of the state's most notable people have been famous politicians. In 1932, Arkansans elected Hattie W. Caraway to fill the Senate seat held by her husband who had died in office. She became the first woman to serve a full term in the United States Senate.

William Jefferson (Bill) Clinton, the forty-second president of the United States, was born in Hope,

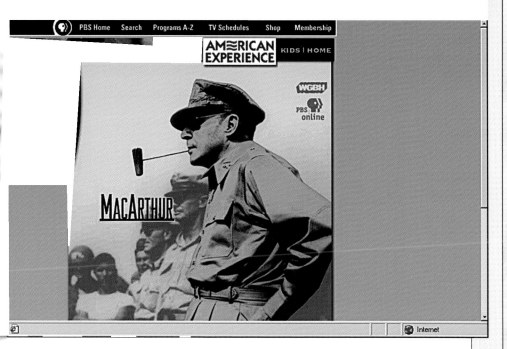

▲ On January 26, 1880, Douglas MacArthur was born in Little Rock, Arkansas. He became one of the United States' leading generals in World War II and the Korean War.

Glen Campbell Biography

Becoming a bona fide living legend isn't as easy as Glen Campbell makes it look. First, you have to have a solid foundation of talent on which to build — like being one of the hottest guitar players in the world. Then you have to record songs that will stand the test of time — standards such as "By The Time I Get To Phoenix" and "Wichita Lineman." And of course, to be a "living" legend, you need to survive the harsh reality of a celebrity lifestyle. Check, check, and check.

Not only do Glen's special appearances as co-headliner at the Andy Williams Moon River Theatre in Branson draw sold-out crowds, but he's still a hot draw on television as well. In 2000, PBS aired a Glen Campbell Special taped in Sioux Falls, SD, and he's been profiled recently on A&E's Biography , VH-1 Behind The Scenes, and CMT's Inside Fame. The CMT profile pulled such strong ratings from the coveted 18-49 demographic that Country Music Television is now showing reruns of the Glen Campbell Goodtime Hour.

Although Glen was already hitting the top of both the country and pop charts by 1969, the Goodtime Hour gave his career "legs." The popular CBS musical variety series was simulcast on the BBC from England to Singapore to Australia and paved the way for five BBC specials. The exposure gave Glen a global presence he enjoys to this day, 30+ years later. He has toured the UK, Europe, Southeast Asia, Australia and New Zealand. As recently as 2000, Glen's popularity in the UK sustained a 31-day tour of the region.

"It's awesome when you think about the power of TV and movies," Glen comments. "If I hadn't had hit

Done   Internet

Glen Campbell was raised in the small town of Billstown, Arkansas. By the age of ten, he had already mastered the guitar—the instrument that would take him to the top of the country and pop charts.

Arkansas. He served as Arkansas attorney general for a few years before being elected governor in 1979. He served as governor from 1979 to 1980, and again from 1982 to 1992. In that time he was successful at improving the state's schools, and attracting new industry and more jobs to the state.

General Douglas A. MacArthur, born in Little Rock, became the supreme commander of Allied Forces in the Pacific during World War II. He later led United Nations forces during much of the Korean War of the 1950s.

Entertainers from Arkansas include country singers Johnny Cash and Glen Campbell, and soul and gospel singer Al Green. Scott Joplin, a composer from Texarkana, became known as the King of Ragtime after he popularized the rhythmic and animated ragtime music.

Actress and author Maya Angelou moved to Stamps, Arkansas, as a young child. She wrote of her difficult childhood in *I Know Why the Caged Bird Sings*. Lawyer and best-selling author John Grisham was born in Jonesboro. He is known for his novels about the legal profession, such as *The Firm* and *The Client*. Many of his books have been made into movies.

Former Chicago Bulls starting forward Scottie Pippen is from Hamburg, Arkansas. He was named by the National Basketball Association as one of the fifty greatest players of all time. Jay Hanna "Dizzy" Dean, from Lucas, was one of baseball's greatest pitchers. He pitched for the St. Louis Cardinals and the Chicago Cubs and was elected to the National Baseball Hall of Fame in 1953.

The state of Arkansas had made great strides in moving into the twenty-first century. Arkansans honor their heritage and take pride in preserving their pioneer way of life. Folk legends and country lifestyles continue to dominate modern-day Arkansas. The state's down-to-earth, homespun way of life has earned one of its cities, Mountain View, the title "Folk Capital of America."

Chapter 2

Land and Climate

The climate of Arkansas makes the state a pleasant place to live throughout the year. Winters in most areas of Arkansas are cool, but not cold. The highlands in the state's north and west experience an average of six inches of snowfall per year, but the temperature on most winter days ranges between 36°F and 42°F. The lowlands enjoy warm, sunny days throughout the winter. Springs are long. Very hot and humid weather usually does not begin until June. In the summer months, temperatures throughout the state average around 80°F. Nighttime temperatures in the mountains are quite cooler, even in the summer.

▲ Rugged hills, thick forests, deep valleys, and swift streams mark Arkansas' Ozark Mountains. These characteristics make this region of Arkansas important to the state's tourism industry. The Ozark Mountains are also significant to the agricultural industry.

Arkansas receives an average of forty-nine inches of rain each year. The Ouachita Mountains see more rainfall than other parts of the state. While abundant rainfall makes droughts rare in Arkansas, tornadoes are commonly experienced. These strong storms most often appear in the Mississippi Valley between the months of March and September.

▶ A Divided State

Arkansas' landscape is divided between the mountainous areas and rich, fertile farmland. If a person was to draw a diagonal line from the northeast corner of the state to the southwest corner, they could see this division. The land to the north and west of the line is the mountainous region. The land to the south and east is where some of the most fertile farmland in the country is located.

▶ Land Regions

Arkansas has five land regions. Little Rock, the state capital, is located where the five land regions meet. The Ozark Plateau, often called the Ozark Mountains, extends into parts of Illinois, Missouri, and Oklahoma. The Ozark Mountains make up the rugged hills, gorges, and valleys of the northwestern and north-central parts of Arkansas. The Ouachita Mountains, extending into Arkansas from Oklahoma, feature parallel ridges and valleys. The thick forests of the Ouachita Mountains yield timber. Deposits of sandstone and limestone are found in these mountains. The hot bubbling springs so often associated with Arkansas are found in the foothills of the Ozark and Ouachita mountains.

Between the Ozark Plateau and the Ouachita Mountains lies the Arkansas Valley, a region of rolling

Magazine Mountain is the highest point in Arkansas at 2,753 feet. This makes it a very popular place for outdoor activities, such as climbing, biking, and hang gliding.

valleys. Although the Arkansas Valley is lowland, the state's highest point, Magazine Mountain, rising 2,753 feet high, is found there. The Arkansas Valley is known for its rich, fertile soil, coal, and natural gas.

The Mississippi Alluvial Plain lies to the west of the Mississippi River and extends the length of the eastern third of the state from Missouri to Louisiana. Alluvial land is also known as the Delta. The soil in the Delta consists of deposits from years of flooding along the Mississippi River. As the floodwaters receded, they left behind layers of rich sediment. The Delta is an important economic and agricultural region. The area is now protected from the Mississippi River's floods by a long system of levees and drainage ditches.

Crowley's Ridge, a group of narrow hills, runs through the central part of the Delta. Gravel deposits and yellow mineral particles called loess make up the ridge.

The West Gulf Coastal Plain is located in the southwestern and south-central parts of Arkansas. It also continues into Louisiana and Texas. This low section of the state is good for farming. It is often called the Timberlands because of its rich pine forests. The West Gulf Coastal Plain has many bayous and swamps. Oil has been found in this area.

Rivers

The Mississippi River runs along the eastern edge of Arkansas and forms the state's border with Tennessee and Mississippi. The course of the Mississippi River has changed over the years so that land that was part of Arkansas is now in Mississippi and Tennessee, and vice versa. The Arkansas River begins in Colorado and enters Arkansas from Oklahoma. It follows a southeasterly course until it flows into the Mississippi River. It is the largest river in Arkansas and the fourth longest river in the United States. The Arkansas River runs through the Arkansas Valley between the Ozark and Ouachita mountains and through the Mississippi Alluvial Plain. A navigation system called the McClellan-Kerr Arkansas River Navigation System, completed in 1970, allows boats to travel the Arkansas River from its mouth at the Mississippi River to Tulsa, Oklahoma.

Every part of Arkansas has a river running through it. In addition to the Arkansas River, the Ouachita River flows through the central part of the Ouachita Mountains in the south-central part of the state. The Red River flows through the southwest corner, the White River through the northern and eastern sections, and the St. Francis

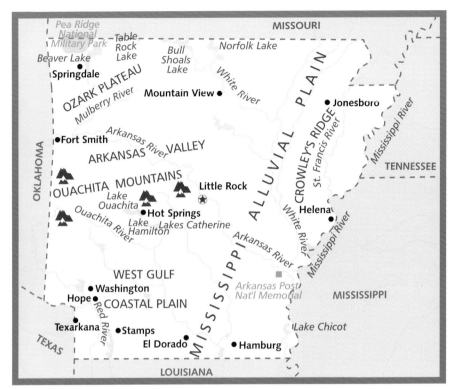

▲ *A map of Arkansas.*

River flows in the eastern part of the state. Arkansas rivers are important for travel and recreation, and river fishing helps the state's economy. Arkansas has 9,700 miles of streams and rivers.

▶ Natural, Artificial, and Oxbow Lakes

Arkansas lakes cover over 600,000 acres.[1] Most are artificial and were created by damming the rivers that cut through the state. The largest natural lake in Arkansas is Lake Chicot, which was formed six hundred years ago when the Mississippi River changed its course. A lake created when a river changes its course is known as an oxbow lake. Lake Chicot is the largest oxbow lake in North

▲ At twenty miles in length, Lake Chicot is the state's largest natural lake and North America's largest oxbow lake. It is very popular for fishing and bird watching. Lake Chicot State Park is located on the lake's north end, providing campsites, picnic areas, and more.

America. In 1927, a flood partially created a natural earth dam, which divided the lake into a large lower lake with blue water and a small upper lake with muddy water. The state of Arkansas completed the dam caused by the flood. Dams built along the Ouachita and Arkansas rivers created a chain of artificial lakes. Lakes Catherine, Hamilton, and Ouachita are located in the Ouachita Mountains. Beaver, Bull Shoals, Norfork, and Table Rock lakes lie along the White River.

Bull Shoals Lake, located in north-central Arkansas, is not only beautiful, but it is a great place to scuba dive, fish, and go boating. ▷

Chapter 3

Economy

Like its neighboring states, Arkansas depended upon the cotton industry for economic stability prior to the Civil War. The fertile soil of the Mississippi Valley, the labor of slaves, and the close proximity of the Mississippi River to transport the cotton to textile mills helped make Arkansas a major cotton-producing state. Over the last 150 years, Arkansas' economy switched from farming to manufacturing. In the 1960s, money made from manufacturing surpassed money made from farming for the first time.

Farming now represents about 6 percent of the total economy. Manufacturing is Arkansas' major economic

▲ Cotton is one of the leading crops in Arkansas. It is grown primarily on the Mississippi Alluvial Plain in the eastern part of the state.

activity. Service industries, jobs that people do that provide a service, make up the largest percentage of the gross state product (GSP). The GSP is the total value of all goods and services produced in the state in one year. Fifty-six percent of Arkansans work in cities in the service industries.

A Farming Society

Not all Arkansans profited from cotton in the mid-1800s. In the hill country, farmers did not bring their crops to market because they grew just enough to live on. This is called subsistence farming. The Civil War hurt the value of many plantations, homes, and businesses in Arkansas. Subsistence farms, or small family farms, continued to exist after the Civil War. Many freed slaves turned to sharecropping—the farming of the owner's land in return for a share of the crops grown. Eventually cotton became the main crop of the plantations once again, but the plantations also grew soybeans and rice. The Industrial Revolution that impacted the rest of the United States at first had little effect on Arkansas.

Moving Toward an Industrial Economy

Late in the 1800s, three things directed Arkansas toward an industrial economy. First, railroad construction began in the state. Mining industries thrived after the discovery of bauxite near Little Rock, and lastly, a demand for wood and other building supplies spurred timber-related industries.

The Arkansas economy could rely even less on farming when the Delta flooded in 1927. A few years later, the state suffered a drought, which further decreased the output of Arkansan farms. The Great Depression followed. During that time, cotton sold for less than it cost to grow. In addition to helping farmers, President Franklin

▲ President Franklin Delano Roosevelt (second from the left) aided the Arkansas economy with his New Deal. Here he visits Hot Springs in 1936.

D. Roosevelt's "New Deal" helped Arkansans recover economically by providing social security, educational support, and modernization of roads, public buildings, and national sites.

In the 1940s, Arkansas helped during World War II by manufacturing food and munitions for the war effort. Farms and factories flourished during this time. It was only after the war that the impact of the Industrial Revolution affected the state, and Arkansas economy switched from agriculture to industry. In 1955, the Arkansas' Industrial Development Commission was formed to attract new manufacturing plants to the state. The gradual switch from an agricultural state to an industrial state left many agricultural workers without jobs. Many farmers left Arkansas during these years.

Food, Paper, and Metal Products

Manufacturing contributes 25 percent to Arkansas' gross state product, and more Arkansans work in manufacturing than in any other industry. Manufacturing is found mostly in the Fort Smith and Little Rock areas. Food processing and the production of canned goods rank high among manufactured products. Poultry, meat, milk, farm animal feed, and soft drinks are among the many food products produced in Arkansas. The world's largest producer and processor of poultry products, Tyson Foods, is located in Springdale. Food processing plants are located throughout Arkansas.

Arkansas' forests produce lumber and paper products. Other manufactured products include refrigeration equipment, metalworking machinery, electrical equipment, and fabricated metal products, such as pipe fittings and valves.

Agriculture

Roughly half of Arkansas is covered with farmland. The state has close to fifty thousand farms. Sixty percent of farm income comes from livestock production, including broilers (young chickens). Arkansas is one of the United States' most important broiler producers. Beef cattle, raised on farms throughout the state, are the second most important livestock product in Arkansas. Hogs, eggs, milk, and turkey also are important to the agricultural economy. Catfish are raised on fish farms and sold for food.

Crops provide 40 percent of the Arkansas farm income. Soybeans are the state's most important crop followed by rice. Arkansas leads the United States in rice production,

Arkansas is the second largest producer of broilers in the United States.

producing almost one third of the nation's crop. The rich soil of the Mississippi Alluvial Plain also supports the growth of cotton, corn, grapes, pecans, and wheat. Hay is grown in northwestern Arkansas.

Mining

Natural gas and petroleum are Arkansas' two leading mineral products. Oil fields have been discovered near El Dorado in the southern part of the state. Bromine, used in the manufacture of chemicals, is mined from brines located in south central Arkansas. Bauxite, a mineral that contains aluminum, is mined near Little Rock. Other mining products include crushed stone, cement, coal, gravel, and gypsum.

A Helping Economy

The service industries are a collective group of businesses that help individuals, industries, and other businesses. They include education, health care, government services, real estate, wholesale and retail trade, and transportation. The service industries employ more workers than any other industry in Arkansas.

Wholesale and retail trade are the state's most important service industries. Wal-Mart stores, Dillard's department stores, and TCBY yogurt stores are three nationally known retail chains based in Arkansas. Second in importance among the service industries is the community, business, and personal services group. This segment of service industries includes private health care, nursing homes, law firms, and auto repair shops.

The state has about ninety-four thousand miles of roads and highways. Passenger and freight trains run through Arkansas. Little Rock is the state's chief financial center as well as its center of transportation. Little Rock also hosts the state's largest airport.

Government services include the operation of Little Rock Air Force Base, the largest military installation in Arkansas.

Education

The Arkansas state budget does not allocate much money for public education, and the number of public schools in Arkansas has decreased over the years.

Arkansas' fifteen public colleges bring money into the state by attracting out-of-state students. The University of Arkansas, with five campuses spread throughout the state, is the largest school of higher education in the state. It is known for its J. William Fulbright College of Arts and Sciences. There are also many private colleges and universities. Arkansas has a system of twenty-three two-year community colleges and technical institutes. Arkansas has one medical school, the University of Arkansas for Medical Sciences, located in Little Rock. The University of Arkansas in Fayetteville is the state's oldest college. It was chartered in 1852.

▷ Tourism

Tourism is important to the Arkansas economy. Its lakes and streams offer many opportunities for sailing, canoeing, waterskiing, boating, and other water sports. The Ouachita Mountains are Arkansas' most-visited location. Lake Chicot and the Arkansas River are well known for recreational fishing. Nature lovers enjoy Arkansas' caves and caverns, such as the Blanchard Springs Caverns located in the Ozark National Forest. The Arkansas Conservation Amendment funds improvements to the state parks to provide recreational opportunities year-round.

Many tourists travel to Arkansas for the hot spring waters, which bubble out of the ground in the foothills of the Ouachita and Ozark mountains. Some springs contain minerals, which many believe will heal certain medical conditions. Mammoth Spring is one of the largest springs in the United States.

◁ *The Mulberry River was declared a National Wild and Scenic River in 1992. As one of Arkansas' wildest rivers, it is a very popular whitewater rafting spot in the spring time. Other activities, such as canoeing, swimming, and floating, are better during the summer months when the river is calmer.*

Tourists also flock to Arkansas for its historic sites. A major Civil War battle is commemorated at Pea Ridge National Military Park, located in the northwestern part of the state. At the Arkansas Post National Memorial, tribute is paid to the first permanent white settlement in Arkansas. Fort Smith National Historic Site is the site of one of the first military posts in the American West. Visitors interested in American Indian history can visit the Toltec Ceremonial Mounds at Toltec Mounds Archaeological State Park, near Little Rock. Archaeological studies continue at the site.

► Arts and Sports

Little Rock is the site of the Arkansas Arts Center and the Arkansas Museum of Science and History. Arkansas State University and the University of Arkansas each have museums, as do a number of Arkansan cities. In the summer, tourists and residents may enjoy river cruises on the Arkansas River or attend the Music Festival of Arkansas. The King Biscuit Blues Festival is held in Helena in October. Folk festivals are held at the Ozark Folk Center in Mountain View, where Arkansas Crafts Guild members sell their crafts. Autumn is the time for the many antique fairs and craft shows that occur throughout the state.

Year-round sports help the Arkansan economy. The spring season brings thoroughbred racing to Oaklawn Park in Hot Springs. The University of Arkansas is home to the football and basketball teams called the Razorbacks. The Arkansas State University's football team is called the Indians. The Arkansas Travelers is a community-owned, minor-league baseball team that has won seven minor-league championships. They play at Little Rock's Ray Winder Field.

File   Edit   View   Favorites   Tools   Help

Address http://www.pbs.org/riverofsong/artists/e3-robert.html

| PBS Home | Search | Programs A-Z | TV Schedules | Shop | Membership |

the River of Song project | the artists | music along the river
calendar | teacher's guide | pressroom | the store

THE MISSISSIPPI
RIVER OF SONG

The Artists

Southern Fusion   1   2   ③   4

Robert Lockwood, Jr.
Helena, Arkansas

Artists by Genre
Artists Alphabetically

Previous Artist
Next Artist

discography
audio/video

Smithsonian Institution

For a lot of people, the Mississippi Delta is virtually synonymous
with the blues. Robert Lockwood, Jr. is part of the generation
that put the Delta on America's musical map. Stepson of the
Delta's most famous early star, Robert Johnson, Lockwood cut

▲ *Arkansas blues artist Robert Lockwood, Jr., returns to his home state
every year to perform at the King Biscuit Blues Festival.*

▷ Planning for the Future

Arkansas leaders work to attract new business to the state,
including foreign and technological businesses. Education
and technical training in Arkansas have been improved
over the years to attract and keep a capable and experienced workforce in the state.

Government

Two United States senators and four members of the United States House of Representatives represent Arkansas in Congress. As of the 2000 race, Arkansas had six electoral college votes in presidential elections. Traditionally, Arkansas voted for the Democratic Party, but the Republican Party gained strength in Arkansas in the 1990s.

The Executive Branch

Arkansas state government is divided into three branches: the executive, legislative, and judicial. The governor serves a term of four years and may not serve more than two terms. A gubernatorial candidate must be a United States citizen, thirty years of age, and a resident of Arkansas for seven or more years. A lieutenant governor, secretary of state, attorney general, treasurer, auditor, and land commissioner are elected by the citizens of Arkansas to run their state government. All of these officials serve terms of four years and may serve no more than two terms. The governor also appoints an adjutant general, controller, and heads of departments and commissions. Some appointees must be approved by the state legislature before being approved for office.

The General Assembly

The state legislature is called the Arkansas General Assembly. The general assembly consists of the state house of representatives and the state senate. It is responsible for

passing the laws of Arkansas. Legislative sessions begin on the second Monday in January in odd-numbered years. The sessions can last as long as sixty calendar days. If approved by a two-thirds vote of both houses, legislative sessions may be continued. The governor may call a special session of the general assembly. There is no time limit on special sessions called by the governor.

Thirty-five state senators, one from each state senatorial district, serve in the general assembly for a term of four years. They can serve no more than two terms. One hundred representative districts each elect one member of the state house of representatives. Members serve two-year terms and cannot serve more than three terms. Representation is based on population. All lawmakers must live in Arkansas for a

▲ *The Arkansas State Capitol Building.*

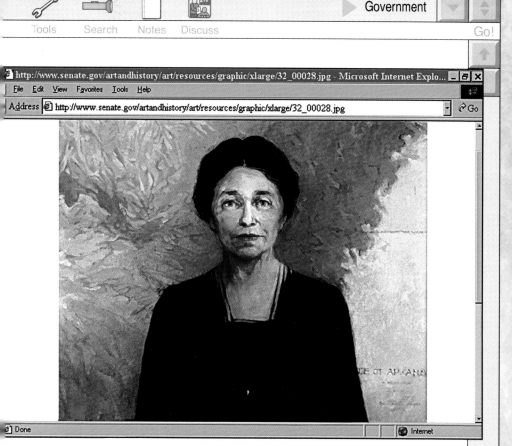

Hattie Ophelia Wyatt Caraway was the first woman ever to be elected to a full term in the U.S. Senate in 1932. She served the remainder of her husband's term as senator from Arkansas.

minimum of two years and in their districts for at least one year before running for office.

The State Constitution

Arkansas has had five state constitutions. The current one was adopted in 1874. Amendments may be made to the constitution in one of three ways. Members of the general assembly can introduce an amendment. These amendments are called legislative amendments. A majority of both the state senate and house of representatives must approve legislative amendments for them to become part

of the state constitution. The second way amendments can be added is by petitions signed by voters. These are called initiative amendments. Amendments can also be proposed by constitutional conventions. A constitutional convention must be called by the voters. Every amendment proposed at a constitutional convention must then be approved by a majority of voters in an election.

The Judicial Branch

Arkansas' highest court is the state supreme court. The chief justice and six associate judges who serve on the supreme court are elected. Each state supreme court judge's term of office is eight years. Residents also elect circuit court judges to six-year terms.[1] Circuit courts hear criminal cases and cases involving monetary damages.

There are seventy-five counties in Arkansas. Each county has a county court with a judge elected to a two-year term. Elected municipal judges preside over the lower courts. The county judge makes decisions regarding county fiscal matters. The county judge also presides over the county quorum court, a court of all the justices of the peace in the county. One of the responsibilities of the quorum court is to approve the county budget.

Local Government

Most cities in Arkansas are governed by a mayor and town council. The capital city of Little Rock uses the manager-council type of government. County officials include the assessor, clerk, coroner, sheriff, surveyor, treasurer, and collector. In some Arkansas counties, the collector also serves as the sheriff.

History

The earliest known inhabitants of the land that is now Arkansas were the Paleo Indians who lived there over twelve thousand years ago. They were a hunting-and-gathering people. Thousands of years later, the Archaic Indians lived in caves in the Ozark region. Their society was more advanced than that of the Paleo Indians, because

The Toltec Mounds - Microsoft Internet Explorer

File   Edit   View   Favorites   Tools   Help

Address http://www.cast.uark.edu/~shelley/html/parkin/toltecmoundpg.html   Go

The Toltec Mounds

In the modern farmlands of the Arkansas River Valley are the remains of a large group of ancient earthworks known as the Toltec Mounds. This impressive archeological site has attracted national interest for over 100 years and was designated a National Historic Landmark in 1978. Toltec Mounds is one of the largest and most complex sites in the Lower Mississippi Valley. Located on the bank of Mound Pond, it once had an earthen embankment on three sides. A century ago, 16 mounds were known inside the embankment and two of them were 38 to 50 feet high. Today, several mounds and a remnant of the embankment are visible and locations of other mounds are known.

The embankment was an impressive earthwork 8 to 10 feet high and 5,298 feet long with a ditch on the outside. Mounds were placed along the edges of two open areas (plazas) which were used for political, religious, and social activities attended by people from the vicinity. Mound locations seem to have been planned using principles based on alignment with important solar positions and standardized units of measurement. Most of the mounds were square or rectangular, flat-topped platforms with buildings on them. Mound B (38'high) was constructed

CLICK HERE
ANIMATION

Internet

▲ Toltec Mounds State Park contains eighteen mounds created by the Mississippian Indians. Made from the earth, these mounds were built to serve as a platform onto which an important building, such as a religious institution or home of an important family, was erected.

they grew food as well as hunted. They were also weavers and basket makers. Around 1000 B.C., a tribe of American Indians known as Mound Builders settled along the Mississippi River. They were given this name because of the huge ceremonial hills they built.

At the time of Hernando de Soto's explorations from 1540 to 1542, there were three tribes of American Indians living in Arkansas. The Osage tribe hunted and trapped animals for food in the Ozark Mountains. The Caddo tribe lived in the western part of the state, and the Quapaw farmers organized their tribes into small villages in eastern Arkansas. Marquette and Joliet encountered friendly Quapaw Indians upon arriving in Arkansas. One French explorer-historian found that "these [Indians] are . . . civil, liberal, and of a gay humor."[1] Fearing hostile Spaniards and American Indians farther south, they did not continue their exploration of the Mississippi River to the Gulf of Mexico.

▶ The Louisiana Purchase

In 1682, the Frenchman René-Robert Cavelier, Sieur de La Salle, led an exploration party of American Indians, French soldiers, and explorers down the Mississippi River to the Gulf of Mexico. La Salle claimed all the land drained by the Mississippi River for France. He named it Louisiana after King Louis XIV. Arkansas Post, settled by the French under Henri de Tonti, became the first European settlement located in the lower Mississippi Valley. It later became the territorial capital of Arkansas.

France ceded Louisiana to Spain in 1762. The Louisiana Territory was held by Spain until 1800, when France, under Napoléon Bonaparte, forced Spain to return it.

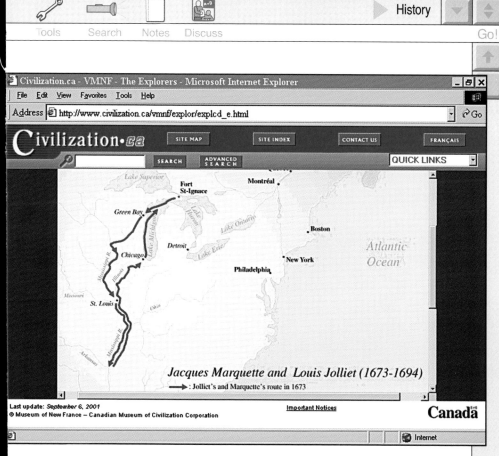

Civilization.ca - VMNF - The Explorers - Microsoft Internet Explorer

File Edit View Favorites Tools Help

Address http://www.civilization.ca/vmnf/explor/explcd_e.html   Go

Civilization·ca   SITE MAP   SITE INDEX   CONTACT US   FRANÇAIS

SEARCH   ADVANCED SEARCH   QUICK LINKS

Jacques Marquette and Louis Jolliet (1673-1694)

→ : Jolliet's and Marquette's route in 1673

Last update: *September 6, 2001*
© Museum of New France – Canadian Museum of Civilization Corporation   Important Notices   **Canada**

Internet

▲ *In 1673, Jacques Marquette and Louis Joliet (also spelled Jolliet) traveled down the Mississippi River to the mouth of the Arkansas River.*

After the Revolutionary War, the Mississippi River became a valuable means of transportation of pioneers, food, household supplies, and other freight. In 1803, Thomas Jefferson purchased the Louisiana Territory from France for $15 million, and the size of the United States doubled.

The northern part of the Louisiana Purchase, including Arkansas, became the Missouri Territory. The southern part was called the Louisiana Territory. In 1819, the United States created the Arkansas Territory from the Louisiana Territory. The newly named area included all of present-day Arkansas, as well as parts of what is now Oklahoma and the Texas panhandle. The more centrally

▲ *Fort Smith, Arkansas.*

located town of Little Rock was selected to replace Arkansas Post as the capital in 1821. Fort Smith, established by the government to keep peace between the various tribes of American Indians and pioneers, became an important supply station for the forty-niners seeking gold in California.

▶ Statehood and Secession

Arkansas was admitted into the Union on June 15, 1836. While the United States grappled with the confusion and turmoil over the issue of slavery, the Arkansas economy thrived. When Abraham Lincoln was elected president in 1860, several Southern states seceded from, or left, the Union. Although a slave state, Arkansas at first did not secede, but refused to send troops to fight the Confederates. In May 1861, Arkansas officially seceded from the United States. Arkansas was divided over the War Between the States—some people from counties in northern Arkansas remained loyal to the Union, while counties in the southern part of the state were pro-Confederate.

Important Civil War battles fought in northwestern Arkansas included Pea Ridge in March 1862, and Prairie Grove in December of the same year. The Union Army was victorious in both battles and they captured Little Rock on September 10, 1863. A Union government was formed in Little Rock and the Confederates set up another capital at Washington, in southwestern Arkansas. The state had both a Union and Confederate government until the end of the Civil War.

Arkansas was readmitted to the Union in 1868. While most of the northern part of the state had been ravaged by war, many of the cotton plantations of the Mississippi Delta continued to thrive. Still, Reconstruction was difficult for Arkansans, who lived under the jurisdiction of federal troops until 1874. Conflict between people of different races and political parties led to bloodshed as Arkansas attempted to regain status as one of the United States.

There was dissension and conflict even between members of the same political party. In 1874, Arkansas nearly came to a state civil war over a rivalry for the office of governor. President Ulysses S. Grant declared Elisha Baxter the governor of Arkansas after his opponent, Joseph Brooks, forced Baxter out of the statehouse at gunpoint.

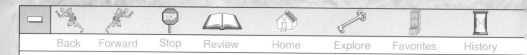
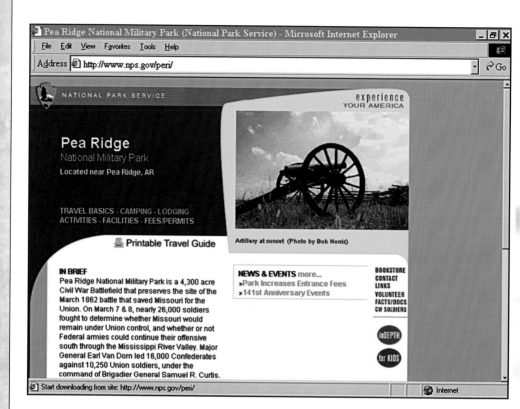

Pea Ridge National Military Park (National Park Service) - Microsoft Internet Explorer

File Edit View Favorites Tools Help

Address http://www.nps.gov/peri/

NATIONAL PARK SERVICE

experience
YOUR AMERICA

Pea Ridge
National Military Park
Located near Pea Ridge, AR

TRAVEL BASICS - CAMPING - LODGING
ACTIVITIES - FACILITIES - FEES/PERMITS

Printable Travel Guide

Artillery at sunset (Photo by Bob Norris)

IN BRIEF
Pea Ridge National Military Park is a 4,300 acre
Civil War Battlefield that preserves the site of the
March 1862 battle that saved Missouri for the
Union. On March 7 & 8, nearly 26,000 soldiers
fought to determine whether Missouri would
remain under Union control, and whether or not
Federal armies could continue their offensive
south through the Mississippi River Valley. Major
General Earl Van Dorn led 16,000 Confederates
against 10,250 Union soldiers, under the
command of Brigadier General Samuel R. Curtis.

NEWS & EVENTS more...
»Park Increases Entrance Fees
»141st Anniversary Events

BOOKSTORE
CONTACT
LINKS
VOLUNTEER
FACTS/DOCS
CW SOLDIERS

inDEPTH

for KIDS

Start downloading from site: http://www.nps.gov/peri/   Internet

△ On March 7 and 8, 1862, Union and Confederate forces battled at what
is now the Pea Ridge National Military Park, in Arkansas. This Union
victory ensured continued federal control of Missouri, as well as the
Union's continued offensive south through the Mississippi River Valley.

▷ Integration at Central High School

Arkansas' recovery from the Civil War was particularly
difficult for the freed slaves and other African-American
citizens in the state. Many Southern states passed "Jim
Crow" laws, which made segregation between the races
mandatory in public places. African Americans could not
eat in the same restaurants, study in the same schools, or
even sit next to a white person on a bus or train. The
United States Supreme Court allowed segregation as long

as the segregated services were "equal" to those provided to whites. In most cases they were not. Segregation was not reduced in Arkansas or elsewhere in the South until the civil rights movement of the 1960s.

The twentieth century brought several changes to Arkansas, as well as to the rest of the country. In May 1954, the United States Supreme Court ruled that segregation violated the Fourteenth Amendment of the Constitution. Segregation in public schools, in particular, was ordered to stop. On September 4, 1957, nine African-American students attempted to enroll in Little Rock's Central High School. In defiance of a ruling by the federal government, Governor Orval Faubus activated the Arkansas National

▲ *Arkansas National Guardsmen direct Elizabeth Eckford away from Little Rock Central High School on September 4, 1957.*

Guard to prevent the students from entering the high school. Angry citizens in favor of segregation supported the governor and aided in the attempt to keep the students from entering. One African-American student selected for integration recalled that going to school each day required her to think of herself as a warrior.[2]

President Dwight D. Eisenhower intervened in the conflict. He put the Arkansas National Guard under federal control, and sent troops from the 101st Airborne Division to Central High School to protect the nine students. He allowed them to attend school for the rest of

▲ *The Little Rock, Arkansas, skyline at dusk.*

the year. In 1958, the high schools in Little Rock were closed but in 1959, a federal court ordered the schools opened and for integration to proceed. This led to the eventual integration of all public schools in the country.

Going Forward

As it moves into the twenty-first century, Arkansas faces different challenges. Pollution, especially water pollution resulting from the poultry industry, is a major problem. More money is needed to strengthen the public school system. Arkansas must find new ways to compete with more technologically-advanced states to bring additional high-tech industry within its borders. Arkansans hope to meet these challenges and overcome them. Like their pioneer ancestors who braved new frontiers, present-day Arkansans will try to forge better lives for themselves and for future generations.

Chapter Notes

Chapter 1. The Natural State

1. Borgna Brunner, ed., *Time Almanac 2003* (Boston: Information Please, 2002), p. 142.

2. Harry S. Ashmore, *Arkansas: A History* (New York: W. W. Norton and Company, 1978), p. 69.

3. Arkansas Department of Parks and Tourism, "Crater of Diamonds," *Arkansas State Parks,* 2002–2003, <http://www.arkansasstateparks.com/parks/default.asp?=parkCrater+of+Diamonds> (April 15, 2003).

Chapter 2. Land and Climate

1. Arkansas Department of Parks and Tourism, "Arkansas Lakes," *Arkansas: The Natural State,* 2003, <http://www.arkansas.com/outdoors_sports/lakes/ (April 15, 2003).

Chapter 4. Government

1. Arkansas Judiciary, "Circuit Court," *Arkansas Judiciary,* 2002, <http://courts.state.ar.us/courts/cir.html> (April 15, 2003).

Chapter 5. History

1. Federal Writers Project. *Arkansas: A Guide to the State* (New York: Hastings House, 1941), p. 30.

2. Melba Pattillo Beals, *Warriors Don't Cry: A Searing Memoir of the Battle to Integrate Little Rock's Central High* (New York: Washington Square Press, 1994), p. xx.

Further Reading

Aylesworth, Thomas G. *South Central: Arkansas, Kansas, Louisiana, Missouri, Oklahoma.* Broomall, Penn.: Chelsea House Publishers, 1995.

DiPiazza, Domenica. *Arkansas.* Minneapolis, Minn.: Lerner Publications, 1994.

Fox, Mary Virginia. *Douglas MacArthur.* Farmington Hills, Mich.: Gale Group, 1999.

Fradin, Dennis Brindall. *Arkansas.* Chicago: Children's Press, 1994.

Greene, Carol. *Bill Clinton: Forty-Second President of the United States.* Danbury, Conn.: Children's Press, 1997.

Kavanagh, James. *Arkansas Birds.* Blaine, Wash.: Waterford Press, 1999.

Kummer, Patricia. *Arkansas.* Minnetonka, Minn.: Capstone Press, Inc., 2003.

McNair, Sylvia. *Arkansas.* Chicago: Children's Press, 2001.

Somerlott, Robert. *The Little Rock School Desegregation Crisis in American History.* Berkeley Heights, N.J.: Enslow Publishers, 2001.

Thompson, Kathleen. *Arkansas.* Austin, Tex.: Raintree/Steck-Vaughn, 1996.